SCANIA BUSES AND COACHES

HOWARD BERRY

AMBERLEY

First published 2022

Amberley Publishing
The Hill, Stroud
Gloucestershire, GL5 4EP

www.amberley-books.com

Copyright © Howard Berry, 2022

The right of Howard Berry to be identified as
the Author of this work has been asserted in
accordance with the Copyrights, Designs and
Patents Act 1988.

ISBN 978 1 4456 7470 4 (print)
ISBN 978 1 4456 7471 1 (ebook)

British Library Cataloguing in Publication Data.
A catalogue record for this book is available from
the British Library.

Origination by Amberley Publishing.
Printed in the UK.

Introduction

ABBA aside, probably the most famous things to come out of Sweden are motor vehicles manufactured by Saab, Volvo or Scania, with the last of these three being the focus of this book. Formed in 1911 through the merger of Södertälje-based Vagnfabriks Aktiebolaget i Södertelge (Vabis) and Malmö-based Maskinfabriks-aktiebolaget Scania, Skåne (or Scania) being the southernmost region of Sweden. Vabis was established in 1891 as a railway car manufacturer while Scania was slightly younger, having been established as a bicycle manufacturer in 1900. Both companies had previously tried building cars, trucks and engines, but with varied success, and by 1910, Vabis was on the brink of bankruptcy. That year, Scania made an offer of takeover to Vabis, and the following year the merger took place, with the former Vabis plant becoming responsible for development and production of engines and light vehicles, and the Scania factory the truck manufacturing facility. Initially the headquarters were located in Malmö, but in 1912 they were moved to Södertälje.

For the first few years, the new company's profits stagnated, maybe because of the decision to build high-class luxury cars (an example being the type III limousine, which had a top hat holder in the roof), but with the outbreak of the First World War everything changed and almost the whole of the company's output was diverted to the Swedish Army, and by 1916 it was making enough profit to invest in redeveloping both of their production facilities. In 1919, the production of cars and buses ceased, Scania deciding to focus completely on truck building. However, when the heavy commercial market was swamped with decommissioned former military vehicles, Scania was unable to compete and in 1921 was declared bankrupt. Following an injection of capital from the wealthy Wallenberg family via their Stockholm's Enskilda Bank, Scania-Vabis was revived and remains a thriving and viable organisation to this day, with production plants in Sweden, Poland, Argentina, India, France, the Netherlands, Brazil, Russia and Finland, as well as assembly plants in a further ten countries across Africa, Asia and Europe.

When Scania-Vabis was formed in 1911, a new logo was created with the head of a griffin (the coat of arms of the Skåne region) surrounded by a three-spoke bicycle chainset. However, for quite some time a 'logo-war' was waged with Daimler-Benz, who claimed possible confusion between the Scania-Vabis design and the Mercedes 'three-pointed star'. In 1968, Daimler-Benz won and the Scania-Vabis logo was changed to a griffin's head on a white background and the bicycle crank removed, and at the same time the company was rebranded as just Scania, Vabis disappearing from the name and logo. A year later there was to be a further name change when Scania merged with Saab, the new company being known as Saab-Scania AB. Saab were based in Trollhättan and were a well-known car and aeroplane manufacturing company. Saab had previously imported Triumph engines to fit into their cars, but the merger meant they could start to use Scania's engine manufacturing facilities and in 1977 took advantage of Scania's experience with turbochargers and created one of the earliest mass-produced turbocharged car engines. In 1990, American automotive giant General Motors purchased a 51 per cent stake in the Saab division, and a year later Investor AB, the holding company of the Wallenberg family, purchased the remaining shares. In 1995, General Motors purchased the remaining Saab shares from Investor AB, and the company was divested, Investor AB retaining the whole of the truck and bus division and renaming it to Scania AB. After a number of aborted takeover attempts in the late 1990s early 2000s, Scania became a wholly owned subsidiary of the Volkswagen Group in 2015 and became part of Volkswagen's heavy commercial vehicle division, Traton SE.

Apart from a brief dalliance with a few Swedish lovelies when working for National Express back in the late 1980s and early 1990s, my Scania connection only really started when I became Area Operations Manager for First Potteries in 2005, a company whose full-sized single-deck fleet was almost 100 per cent Scanias. The buses were reliable, comfortable, lovely to drive and well-liked by the drivers, and I soon became a great admirer of the Scania, and would more than happily get 'behind the wheel' whenever the opportunity arose. This book takes you through the life of Scania in the United Kingdom and Ireland year by year from the first arrivals to the latest models and contains 180 colour pictures with (hopefully) informative and sometimes humorous captions. As with my previous publications I have been greatly assisted in my endeavours by a handful of photographers to whom I am indebted, not only for letting me use their work, but also for having the foresight to record these vehicles in their heyday for others to enjoy so many years later. Each photographer has an initialled credit after their work: Alan Snatt (AS), Martyn Hearson (MH), Richard Simons (RS) and Paul Green (PG). Finally, talking of initials, within the photo captions NBC refers to the National Bus Company, and SBG to the Scottish Bus Group.

Howard Berry, Cheswardine, Shropshire

The 1970s – 'Arrival'

In the last months of 1969, Birmingham-based bodybuilder Metro-Cammell Weymann (MCW) collaborated with Scania to produce the Metro-Scania, a rear-engined semi-integral citybus. Initially, two demonstration vehicles were built, based on Scania's BR110MH chassis and fitted with Scania bodyshells, MCW providing the seating, doors, windows and interior trim. VWD 451H was a forty seater with room for twenty-one standees and was sent to London Transport where it received several minor, but unspecified modifications prior to entering service, while VWD 452H seated thirty-one with room for thirty-eight standees and spent time with Newport and Leicester, both purchasing some of the first production vehicles. The first twenty-five Metro-Scanias were delivered in the same manner as the two prototypes, MCW only providing the doors and internal fittings, but from 1972 MCW assembled the bodies, which were fitted to front and rear sub-assemblies carrying the suspension, axles, engine and gearbox. Including demonstrators, 133 Metro-Scanias were delivered, all but three (for King Alfred Motor Services of Winchester) going to major operators. While the Metro-Scania was popular with those who drove and rode them, thanks to systems like full air suspension, power steering and an asymmetrical windscreen, deeper on the nearside and designed to give the driver a better view of the kerb, they were also rather thirsty as well as costly to buy. With a complete bus starting at nearly £9,000, and with the Leyland National as its nearest competitor (ruling out sale to NBC subsidiaries as the National was a joint venture between the NBC and Leyland) the writing was on the wall, and in 1973 the last Metro-Scanias were delivered. London Transport, who, despite being the first operator to trial the Metro-Scania, ordered no more until receiving the final six as part of a comparison trial, ironically against the National.

Just as Metro-Scania production was ending, Scania and MCW announced another collaboration: the double-deck Metropolitan. Also based on the BR111DH chassis and fitted as standard with full air suspension and power steering, its turbocharged engine made it a lively performer, especially when most rear-engined double-deckers at the time were fitted with reliable but leisurely Gardner or Leyland engines. Like the Metro-Scania, it too was very thirsty, but its Achilles heel was corrosion, and despite MCW attempting numerous anti-corrosion measures, severe problems with their body structure led to most Metropolitans having relatively short first-service lives.

The prototype, NVP 533M, was used as a demonstrator before being sold to West Midlands PTE, a major customer of the local MCW factory. Despite taking large numbers of MCW-bodied Daimler Fleetlines and Bristol VRs, WMPTE showed little interest in the Metropolitan and when only three years old it was sold to Trathens of Yelverton and used on a round London sightseeing contract. The majority of Metro-Scania operators also bought Metropolitans, with London Transport taking over 160 between 1975 and 1977. However, corrosion and reliability issues saw them all withdrawn by 1983. While no NBC subsidiary ordered Metro-Scanias, Maidstone & District received five Metropolitans in 1975 as part of a comparison trial against the Bristol VR and Volvo's Ailsa. Despite favourable reports, the Metropolitan and Ailsa lost to the Bristol VR, which was no surprise as it was already the NBC's standard double-decker. Metropolitan production ended in 1978, the last examples going to Reading Transport, including two with high-speed rear axles to operate the X1 service between Reading and London. Altogether 663 Metropolitans were built, all delivered to British municipal, PTE or nationalised operators. However, the independent sector were quick to snap up these relatively low mileage, modern buses, and some did go on to have long lives with their new owners.

Scania and MCW did build one further vehicle for the home market in the 1970s and that was the unique CR145 coach. Powered by a rear-mounted 14-litre V8 engine producing 260 bhp and fitted with a semi-automatic gearbox, HOM 682L was built in Sweden and finished at MCW's Washwood Heath factory. Fitted with thirty-seven seats and a toilet, it was intended as a luxury intercity express coach, and as such spent some time on loan to the NBC for use on National Travel work. Again, its high price and thirst for fuel prevented further sales in the UK.

Above: For over fifty years, King Alfred Motor Services operated a network of stage carriage services from their base in Winchester. A combination of rising costs and declining passenger numbers saw the company sold to Hants & Dorset in 1973. The final vehicles delivered were three Metro-Scanias, delivered new in 1971. They were the only examples sold to an independent operator. Brand new AOU 108J is seen in Basingstoke bus station. (AS)

Left: NVP 533M, the first Metropolitan, spent its early life on demonstration duties, firstly doing the rounds of the motor shows before being loaned to prospective purchasers. Seen here still in motor show guise and original dual-door configuration, it was subsequently converted to single door before entering regular passenger service. (AS)

The first twenty-five production Metro-Scanias were built with Scania body frames, with twenty of them being delivered to Leicester City Transport in 1971, making them the first operator to put a Metro-Scania into service. 145 (WBC 145J) from that batch is seen with sister ship 219 (ARY 219K) in Abbey Park Road depot in 1974. (AS)

Leicester also received the first production Metropolitans when eight, including 271 (PJF 271M), arrived in early 1974. Again, Abbey Park Road depot is the location, and this nearside view, complete with a happy upper-deck passenger, shows the side-mounted radiators that allowed the downstairs glazing to run the entire length of the lower deck. (AS)

This has been included to allow comparison between the Metropolitan and its successor from the MCW factory, the Metrobus. The family resemblance can clearly be seen: the Metrobus originally retained the asymmetrical windscreen and the side window layout is almost identical. Leicester again where Metropolitan 272 (PJF 272M) and Metrobus 38 (FUT 38V) are seen. (RS)

Another Leicester comparison shot, this time of two Metropolitans, both now wearing the later Leicester City Bus red and white livery, albeit with differing fleet name styles. Native example 299 (GJF 299N) compares with 153 (KJD 206P), formerly London Transport MD6, the single chrome trim on 153 looking more aesthetically pleasing than the double trim on 299. (RS)

In 1972, SELNEC PTE ordered eight long Metro-Scanias for comparison trials with the Leyland National, followed a year later by five shorter-length examples of each model. Despite the Metro-Scania's breathtaking acceleration, their poor fuel consumption saw the National win the day, and no more were ordered. They had relatively long lives up north, all transferring to Leigh depot and remaining in service until the mid-1980s. 1344 (TXJ 517K), originally EX44, is seen waiting time in its home town. (MH)

Despite being one of the largest users of the Metrobus, SELNEC's successor Greater Manchester PTE only ordered ten Metropolitans, as at the time, GMPTE had standardised on the Leyland Atlantean/Daimler Fleetline. They were originally purchased to operate the 400 Trans-Lancs Express service between Bolton and Stockport and so were allocated to my 'local' garage, Tameside. 1430 (GNC 282N) is seen in Ashton-under-Lyne bus station in 1975. (AS)

Newport Borough Council ran the biggest Metro-Scania fleet, with forty-four bought new and a handful purchased second hand from London Transport. They obviously made an impression as by the 1980s, Newport operated the largest Scania fleet in the UK. New in 1972, 53 (YDW 753K) is seen nestled among the Bristols in Newport bus station in 1974. (AS)

The Metropolitan didn't feature anywhere near as strongly as the Metro-Scania in Newport's fleet, with only ten, all delivered in 1975. There's probably a good chance that the denim products sold by Bona-Toggs outlasted the buses as the dreaded Metropolitan corrosion ensured they had pretty short lives in South Wales. Seen in Newport bus station, 114 (GKG 35N) was the first Newport bus to carry an overall advert. (RS)

Above and below: Not only was Merseyside PTE's livery the reverse image of Newport's, their Metro-Scania/Metropolitan order was as well, with only a handful of Metro-Scanias, but one of the largest fleets of Metropolitans. Merseyside initially had separate liveries for its operating divisions, and seen wearing the blue and cream Wirral Division livery is 4002 (CKD 402L) and in the green and cream North/South Division livery is 4013 (CKD 413L). (RS)

The determined-looking rider of the Honda Step-Thru might have easily overtaken the Merseyside Leyland PD2, but the Metropolitan's legendary turn of speed might have proved more of a challenge to him. Still wearing Merseyside's original green and cream livery, 4039 (RKA 439N) is seen at Liverpool's Pier Head in 1975. (AS)

One more livery to appear on Merseyside PTE's Metropolitans was when 4050 (HWM 50P) received Liverpool Corporation Tramways livery in 1979. This was to celebrate fifty years of Merseyside Transport's Edge Lane works, and six vehicles received liveries of the former municipal undertakings which made up the PTE. Looking at the two signs above the back of the bus, I can't confirm whether the Metropolitan's cabs were yellow, but as for Rotters, I think we're safe on that score. (MH)

Above and below: In 1971, London Country launched the Stevenage Superbus using a fleet of Oxford blue and Canary yellow liveried single-deckers on a high frequency network between Stevenage town centre and the housing estates of the Hertfordshire new town. The buses were a mixture of AEC Swifts, Leyland Nationals and new Metro-Scanias including MS3 (JPH 68K), seen when brand new waiting to depart Stevenage for Chells. So popular did Superbus become that in 1973 the three ex-King Alfred Metro-Scanias were acquired from Hants & Dorset, and a rather down-at-heel MS 7 (AOU 110J) is also seen in Stevenage. By 1979 all had been withdrawn and sold for scrap. (AS)

In 1973, to find an alternative to their unreliable AEC Swifts and Merlins, London Transport trialled six Metro-Scanias against six Leyland Nationals on the S2 route between Clapton Pond and Bromley station. So lively were the Metro-Scanias that on the first day of operation, one of them actually ended up in Clapton Pond. Again, the National won the day, and the Metro-Scanias were put into store before being sold to Newport. MS5 (PGC 205L) is seen at Clapton Pond in 1974. (AS)

It wasn't just single-deck buses that LT was having trouble with, as the DMS class Daimler Fleetlines were also proving unreliable. Having gained experience from operating their handful of Metro-Scanias, and as many of the DMSs were bodied by MCW, LT decided to order 164 Metropolitans for delivery between 1975 and 1977. MD116 (OUC 116R) is seen approaching Parliament Square in Westminster on a 53 working to Camden Town. Note the conductor standing by the driver. (AS)

There's something about photos of London in the 1970s that brings back childhood memories of watching TV programmes such as *Grange Hill*, *The Professionals*, and *Minder*. Sadly, by the time these iconic shows were in their heyday, LT's Metropolitans were already on their way out, the first ones being stripped for spares when less than four years old. MD3 (KJD 203P) crosses Vauxhall Bridge in 1976, hotly pursued by a proper Routemaster. (AS)

The only National Bus Company subsidiary to operate the Metropolitan was Maidstone & District, who received five in 1976. They were part of a one-year trial alongside five Ailsas and four Bristol VRs. Detailed reports on fuel and oil consumption, maintenance work and comments by drivers and maintenance staff were made. Despite receiving favourable comments, the British Leyland-owned Bristol VR became the NBC's standard double-decker. 5254 (KKO 254P) is seen in Ore near Hastings when brand new. (AS)

Above and below: Despite the MCW factory being in Washwood Heath, and the company being a major purchaser of MCW bodywork on Daimler and Bristol chassis, West Midlands PTE only purchased one example each of the Metro-Scania and Metropolitan. The Metro-Scania was purchased new, and its lively performance made it ideal for the 993 Airport Express service. It is seen on that very duty in Birmingham having just come past the Camp Hill flyover on Bordesley High Street, a view hardly recognisable now. The Metropolitan, however, has been seen before, being NVP 533M, the former MCW demonstrator. WMPTE acquired it in 1977 after it had been converted to single door and had the staircase moved forward to be above offside the front wheel. If the previous picture was barely recognisable, the location of the Metropolitan wearing its Queen's Silver Jubilee livery has changed beyond all recognition – it's actually Birmingham New Street. (Joe Moriarty collection)

For many years, Merthyr Tydfil Corporation didn't use route numbers, so the empty blind compartments and front-end damage contribute to Metro-Scania 187 (KHB 187L)'s rather down-at-heel look. One of a pair purchased in 1973, it is surprising how shabby the bus actually looks, as when photographed in Merthyr bus station, it was less than a year old. (AS)

The last Metro-Scania, and the only one to receive an 'M' suffix registration, was ordered by Pontypridd UDC. By the time it was delivered, the 1974 local government reorganisation saw Pontypridd become Taff Ely District Council, with the buses renamed accordingly. MCW must have run out of Metro-Scania badges as the bus was delivered carrying Metropolitan badges on the front and sides. (RS)

Above and below: North of the border, only Greater Glasgow PTE purchased new Metropolitans. It was unfortunate that the Metropolitan was launched at the same time as Volvo introduced the Ailsa, an extremely economical double-decker, the majority of which were built entirely in Scotland. I have my suspicion as to which of these two factors made the Ailsa more appealing to Scottish operators than the thirsty Metropolitan. Glasgow's forty Metropolitans arrived in 1974/5 and all had been withdrawn by 1982. M29 (JUS 749N) is seen passing the long-closed VEGA on Glasgow's Union Street as it turns into Argyle Street at the end of its journey. Seen parked on Cadogan Street, M39 (JUS 759N) displays 'Trans-Clyde' lettering, an initiative introduced by the PTE to integrate Glasgow's train, subway and bus services. However, as seen on the front of the bus, GGPTE adopted a no-change policy, which didn't go down well with Glaswegians. When the 1980 Transport Act abolished the Glasgow boundary, passengers found they could travel on Scottish Bus Group vehicles for local journeys, and as the SBG gave change, passengers voted with their feet. (AS/MH)

Above and below: West Yorkshire PTE was created on April Fool's Day 1974 by merging the fleets of Bradford City Transport, Leeds City Transport, and the Huddersfield and Halifax Joint Omnibus Committees. Among the first vehicles purchased by the new undertaking were a batch of Metropolitans including 2612 (HUA 563N). New in 1975, it became the last Metropolitan to operate with WYPTE, not being withdrawn until 1985 and is seen on Cheapside in Bradford. WYPTE eventually ordered ninety-five Metropolitans, with 2685 (RYG 685R) one of the last. It was one of the final vehicles to be painted in the original WYPTE livery with three stripes either side of the destination box. Found to be time-consuming to apply, in 1977 the design was changed to that seen in the photo above. (RS)

South Yorkshire PTE didn't rate the Metropolitan anywhere near as much as their fellow Tykes in the west, and after taking four in 1975, decided to order a large batch of Ailsas instead. With the early morning sun trying to show some enthusiasm to rise over the back of Doncaster depot, the four are seen here lined up in number order. All are fitted with the Videmat self-service ticketing system. Howeverr, 503 appears to have not been fitted with any passenger instruction stickers over the front door. (RS)

Tyne & Wear PTE operated the largest fleet of Metropolitans outside London, taking 140 between 1975 and 1977, all operating out of the Newcastle division. The steering on the first ten was so light that they had to be modified as drivers refused to take them out. One of the later batch, 750 (LBB 750P) is seen passing the County Hotel opposite Newcastle Central Station. (AS)

Above and below: Hull is famed for being the only UK town with its own telecom company, and – trivia alert – in 1989 it introduced the UK's first fully digital telephone network, just in time for all the calls lamenting the withdrawal of Hull's Metropolitans! Between 1975 and 1978, Hull bought thirty new examples, and then added six ex-Merseyside and (for spares only), one of the SYPTE examples. Following deregulation, they were withdrawn en masse in August 1986. Proudly advertising the telephone system is 431 (PKD 431M), seen in the now demolished Lombard Street Central Garage, while 405 (JAG 405N) has a pair of East Yorkshire Motor Services Leyland Atlanteans for company. (RS)

Above and below: Reading Transport's first Metropolitan was a solitary example purchased in 1975. They waited two years before buying a further thirty-two including the final one built. Along the way, they purchased twenty-one second-hand examples from LT (who repainted them for Reading at Aldenham Works) and a further fourteen from Tyne & Wear. First and last are pictured here, 1 (GRX 1N) seen prior to entering service when brand new, and 133 (SGM 133S), parked at Aldgate's Minories bus station in London after having worked the X1 express service. It was one of two fitted with an uprated engine, higher ratio differential and coach-style seating for operating the X1. (AS)

The ex-LT Metropolitans were either sold straight for scrap after less than eight years' service or sold for further service where they had surprisingly long second lives. One such beast was KJD 216P, the former MD16. Withdrawn in 1982 when only six years old, it passed to Guide Friday where it was quickly put to work on 'The Shakespeare Connection' tour of Stratford-upon-Avon. It is seen here parked on Bridge Street in Stratford outside the narrowest McDonald's I've ever been in. (RS)

Now for a real one-off! HOM 682L was the final collaboration between Scania and MCW. Its unique thirty-seven-seat body was built by Scania and finished by MCW. It was mounted onto a rear-engined Scania CR145 chassis fitted with a semi-automatic gearbox and 14.2-litre V8 engine producing a massive (for the time) 260 bhp. Initially loaned to the National Bus Company, a combination of its high purchase price and guzzling fuel consumption saw it remain a one off. It ended its operational days with Carr's Coaches of Silloth, and was sadly scrapped at the start of the millennium. (AS)

The 1980s – 'Take A Chance On Me'

With the end of Metropolitan production, MCW and Scania went their separate ways: MCW with the fully integral Metrobus, a design incorporating a number of features carried over from the Metropolitan, and Scania with the BR112DH chassis. Available in two lengths, 9.5 metres and 10.2 metres, and powered by the 11-litre DN11 engine (and later the turbocharged DS11 engine), it was coupled to either a Scania three-speed or Voith fully automatic gearbox. The first chassis, MUT 265W, arrived in the UK in 1980 and after fitment with an East Lancs body spent time on demonstration duties before being delivered to Leicester City Transport. Despite ordering large batches of the previous generation of Scanias, this was Leicester's only BR112DH. Only thirty-seven BR112DHs were delivered to the UK, Newport Transport being the biggest customer with twenty-nine including nine with Wadham Stringer bodies, the only single-deck BR112DHs. The balance of deliveries included two with Alexander RH bodies for Tyne & Wear PTE, two with Northern Counties bodies for Greater Manchester PTE, one with an East Lancs body for Nottingham and two further demonstrators delivered directly to Scania. In 1984 Scania redesignated chassis numbers, with the BR112DH becoming the N112DH, and surprise surprise, Newport was the first operator to take the model, sixteen split equally between Alexander and East Lancs. A higher proportion of N112DHs were bodied as single-deckers, possibly the most unusual being the batch fitted with Van Hool semi-coach bodies for use on hotel shuttles around Heathrow Airport.

The 1980s saw the start of Scania's major inroad into the UK coaching scene. In 1982, two Jonckheere-bodied BR116s were imported. Fitted with rear-mounted 11-litre engines, DVV 526X was the only 'X' plate Scania coach and the pair were also the only Jonckhere Bermuda-bodied Scanias, subsequent deliveries being fitted with the Bermuda's replacement, the Jubilee. Delivered in Scania demonstration livery, it passed to Armstrong Galley, Tyne & Wear PTE's coaching division, who liked the livery so much they adopted it as their own. The coaches were imported by Roeselare, a new dealership based in Northampton who became Jonckeere's sole UK importer, Roeselare being the Belgian town where Henri Jonckheere started his carriage building business in 1881. The BR116 was replaced by the K112 in late 1982, and in 1983, the first full year of Scania coach chassis being imported into the UK, nearly thirty entered service with operators such as Derek Randall of London, who ordered fifteen for Continental shuttle work. In 1985, the first K92s arrived in the UK. Fitted with 9.2-litre longitudionally mounted rear engines, the majority were bodied as single-deck buses or coaches. However, East Lancs bodied four double-deckers, two of which seated ninety-two passengers, making them the highest capacity buses on the road at the time. Towards the end of the 1980s the K92 and K112 were superseded by the K93 and K113, and by the end of the decade over 600 Scania chassis had been delivered to UK and Irish operators, Scania having firmly entrenched themselves in the market due to the reliability, comfort and quality of their products.

Despite its livery, East Lancs-bodied BR112DH MUT 265W was actually owned by Leicester City Transport but was loaned to Scania for quite some time to act as a demonstrator. It is seen here with Eastbourne Buses at Langney District Shopping Centre in 1981. After use by Leicester it was exported to Singapore. (AS)

The BR112 was never a common model. Operators were understandably reluctant to commit themselves to a new make and model before seeing how someone else fared with it. Only Newport took them in any number, taking twenty-nine out of the thirty-seven UK deliveries. Marshall-bodied 91 (JBO 91W) is seen when brand new, in the company of another Scania, a 110 tractor unit. (RS)

Twenty of Newport's BR112DHs were Marshall-bodied double-deckers, and one way or another, they all ended up with Black Prince of Morley who went on to be the largest independent Scania operator in Britain. JBO 92W, sister ship to the previous picture, is seen here whizzing down Infirmary Street in Leeds. (RS)

The other nine of Newport's BR112DHs were the only single-deck examples delivered to a UK operator and were fitted with Wadham Stringer Vanguard bodies. Several of them also ended up with Black Prince including 14 (RUH 14Y). It is seen heading up Eastgate in Leeds, carrying the Leeds Suburban livery used on a number of Black Prince vehicles. (AS)

The colours on Tyne & Wear PTE's 1 JVK might look similar to those in the picture on page 25, as it too started life as a demonstrator, this time for Roeselare, the UK's first Jonckheere dealership. It was new as DVV 526X, one of only two BR116 chassis imported into the UK, both of which were also the UK's only Jonckheere Bermuda-bodied Scanias. Tyne & Wear liked the colours so much they adopted them for their Armstrong Galley coaching unit. (AS)

Numerically, CEG 60Y was the first of the two B116s, having both chassis and body numbers one lower than DVV 526X, but DVV was registered a few weeks earlier, and so became the only 'X' plate Scania coach. Crusader Travel was linked to Peterborough United Football Club (to whom the coach was registered), so presumably acted as their team coach when required. (AS)

The first of what would be Scania's breakthrough chassis into the UK coach market, the K112, were delivered in 1983 and were also bodied by Jonckheere, but this time with the new Jubilee range. The first fifteen were fitted with Jubilee P50s and delivered to Derek Randall of North London and included DLX 31Y. It is seen here outside The Red Fox Inn at Kerry Bog Village in southern Ireland, now with Devon operator Hookway's of Meeth, and registered 7105 HP. (PG)

The one-piece flat glass upper-deck windscreen only accentuates the already angular look of the East Lancs body fitted to BR112DH EMJ 560Y. This was Scania's own demonstration vehicle, and is seen here being overtaken by two icons of 1980s motoring, a MK3 Ford Capri and Skoda Estelle. With the sea in the background and tramlines in the road, this can only be Blackpool. When its demonstration days were over it became number 395 in the Nottingham City Transport fleet. (RS)

It was once notoriously difficult for manufacturers to make inroads into the Greater Manchester fleet, as for years GM standardised on the Daimler Fleetline and Leyland Atlantean. However, by the early 1980s, other marques started to appear, notably the MCW Metrobus. Two BR112DHs were delivered in 1983, the only ones fitted with Northern Counties bodywork. They were allocated to Leigh depot, but when photographed 1462 (FWH 462Y) was at Atherton in the company of South Yorkshire PTE's Doncaster Transport-liveried Alexander-bodied Leyland Atlantean. For 'one-off' chassis, they had surprisingly long lives in Manchester. (RS)

The majority of the K112 chassis delivered to the UK in the first five years of production were fitted with Jonckheere bodies. These included twelve for the aptly named Birmingham firm of Flights, who operated a network of services between the major airports under the 'Flightlink' banner. Seen loading in central Manchester is B700 EOF, fitted with the low-driver version of the Jubilee range, the P599. (RS)

One of the big players in the Continental coach holiday boom of the early 1980s was Nord Afrik Travel, or NAT Holidays as they became. Already having operated DAFs and Volvos fitted with Jonckheere bodies, in 1985 they took delivery of six tri-axle K112TRSs fitted with the double-deck variant of the Jubilee, the P99. One of them was the Roeselare demonstrator at the 1985 Brighton Coach Rally, although which one is a mystery, as when they were put on the road they were registered B501–B506 GBD. The number attached to the coach in the picture was never issued by the DVLA. (AS)

By 1985 a handful of bodybuilders other than Jonckheere had built on the K112 for the UK, with Plaxton having built the most, but even this only amounting to twenty-two vehicles. An early 1985 delivery was Paramount 3500-bodied 687 DEW, new in May 1985 to Dew's of Somersham, but seen here registered KAZ 4524 with Ausden Clark of Leicester. (RS)

Plaxton's Paramount 4000 was an impressive beast, and looked even more so when in the striking yellow and blue Scottish Citylink livery, gaining it more than one admiring glance from the drivers in the vicinity of Western Scottish K112TRS 213 (C213 BOS). The coach is seen in 1986 when brand new, parked outside the inspectors' offices at London Victoria coach station. (AS)

The only operator to specify bus-bodied K112s was British Airways, who ordered twenty for use on interterminal shuttles at Heathrow and Gatwick. Eleven were fitted with East Lancs bodies, but the first nine, delivered in 1986, had Plaxton Bustlers. When with BA they had a centre door on both sides, but after withdrawal most were rebuilt to front entrance layout. C933 VLB was one such rebuild and is seen here in the ownership of Independent of Horsforth, a subsidiary of Thornes of Bubwith. (PG)

Dutch bodybuilder Berkhof was a relative newcomer to the UK market, the first examples not arriving until 1982 through Essex-based dealers Ensign, but they rapidly found their way into some high-profile fleets such as King's Ferry, Trathens and Green Line. The Esprit, with its simple lines and 'happy' front end styling, was the standard height single-decker, seen here in Brighton in the ownership of Heyfordian of Upper Heyford. Registered as 9467 MU, it was new in 1986 to West Kingsdown Coaches as C829 LJN. (PG)

To my eyes, Berkhof's double-deck offering, the Eclipse, didn't seem as aesthetically pleasing as other double-deck models, and certainly not as pleasant as the Esprit, looking almost as through the top deck was a bit of an afterthought. C591 KTW was one of a pair of K112CRS-bodied Eclipses new to Ebdon's of Sidcup in 1986, and was an entrant at the 1986 British Coach Rally at Brighton. (AS)

The smaller engined K92 was introduced to the UK in 1986, but by the time it was replaced three years later, only fifty-three had been delivered. New to Jones of Login, this rather startled-looking East Lancs-bodied K92, D727 GDE, had made its way to the Yeadon-based Rhodes Coaches fleet. Seen parked in Leeds Central bus station, it had 2+2 seating at the front, and 2+3 at the rear. (AS)

As well as being Berkhof dealers, Ensign also operated a network of tendered London Buses routes in East London before selling out to Hong Kong-based Citybus in 1990. The resultant company, Capital Citybus, operated a pair of East Lancs-bodied K92s delivered new to Kettlewell of Retford, and 764 (D164 UTO) is seen on St Edward's Way, Romford. (AS)

Only four double-deck K92s were built, two for Maidstone Boro'line and two for Grey Green, all fitted with East Lancs bodies. The extended rear overhang created by the engine bay meant that the two Maidstone buses could seat a whopping ninety-two passengers, making them the highest capacity buses in the UK at the time. 213 (D213 MKK) is seen in its home town. (RS)

With Scanias being rear engined, when bodied as buses there was a noticeable step up at the rear to accommodate the engine, as seen on Alexander PS-bodied K92 E25 ECH. New to Derby City Transport, by the time it was captured turning off Morledge into Derby bus station, Derby City Transport had become part of transport giant Arriva. (AS)

Known locally as 'the green buses', AA Motor Services was one of the famous Ayrshire co-operatives, formed by several smaller operators pooling together under one operating name. Latterly, the major operator in AA was Dodd's of Troon, who operated the bus network until June 1997 before selling it to Stagecoach Western Buses in order to concentrate on their coaching activities. Ten years earlier they purchased a pair of East Lancs-bodied N112s, and E76 RCS is seen turning into Ayr bus station. Scania N112CRB East Lancs B51F AA. (AS)

Boro'line was formed in 1986 as an arm's length company of Maidstone Borough Council, and was one of the earliest participants in the London Transport route tendering system. To operate the newly won routes, they ordered fourteen Leyland Lynxes but only eleven arrived in time, so two Alexander-bodied N112s including 702 (E702 XKR) arrived at short notice, hence the 'dealer white' livery. This rapid expansion, as well as competition closer to home, saw Boro'line Maidstone placed into administration in February 1992. (AS)

Back in the 1980s and 1990s, there weren't many Scanias on the National Express network, most operators preferring the Volvo B10M or Leyland Tiger (two examples of which can be seen in this photograph). The most prolific operator was Yorkshire Traction, who used new and second-hand examples fitted with both Plaxton and Van Hool bodies. Seen on Buckingham Palace Road about to enter London Victoria coach station is Paramount 3500-bodied K112 69 (E69 WWF). (AS)

The other main Scania operator on National Express was the newly privatised Wessex of Bristol, the largest operator on the network. They went on a buying spree shortly after being privatised, and as well as National Express-liveried Scanias, added some to the private hire fleet. Turning onto Buckingham Palace Road, ironically while working a National Express service, is Van Hool Alizee-bodied K112 140 (E665 YDT). (AS)

Well-known London coach company Grey-Green commenced London bus operations under tendering in 1986. By 1988 they had become well established, and when a strike at London Country North East saw Grey-Green gaining some of their tendered routes, new vehicles were required. Six East Lancs-bodied N112DRBs arrived in March 1988 to work the 125 route from Winchmore Hill to Finchley Central, including 110 (E110 JYV), seen in Whetstone when brand new. (AS)

Van Hool Alizee-bodied E219 FLD was new to Capital of West Drayton for use on Heathrow Airport terminal shuttle work. One of a batch of twenty-three, they were unusual in having coach bodies mounted on N112DRB bus chassis. Reputed to be rather lively performers due to their variomatic transmission, they were built without luggage lockers, but instead had large luggage pens inside the door. (MH)

New in 1988 to Wessex of Bristol as E252 LAE, Plaxton Paramount 4000-bodied K112TRS RJI 8605 was originally part of the private hire fleet. After breaking down on its first trip abroad (while still picking up its passengers), concerns over misuse of its CAG gearbox saw it in the care of two regular drivers, who would even take it on test runs after servicing. After transfer to the National Express fleet, it moved down the road to join Bakers Dolphin in Weston-super-Mare, with whom it is seen in Trafalgar Square in 1997. (PG)

As I sit writing this in middle of a scorching hot July, I thought I'd include this view of Brighton & Hove's East Lancs-bodied N112DRB 706 (E706 EFG) in Eastbourne in 1991. One of the first of over 200 Scanias to join the Brighton fleet, maybe the snow was the reason for what must have been a rather quick pre-driving check that day – one head and sidelight being out. I'll bet the driver made sure the cab heater was working though. (PG)

Even though Nottingham City Transport took delivery of one of the first BR112s in 1981, it was 1989 before they bought any more new Scanias but then the floodgates opened, and since then nearly 500 have entered the fleet. A number of second-hand examples were also operated including Alexander RH-bodied N112 E307 EVW, new to Harris of Greys in 1988. (AS)

Despite its name, Scancoaches of North Acton's only link with Scania was operating some as part of the fleet – the name reflecting the Scandinavian heritage of Scancoaches' chairman. The VIP Club consisted of three vehicles to full executive specification, primarily for use on football team coach work, Scancoaches holding the Crystal Palace FC contract. Seen in Brighton when brand new is Jonckheere Deauville-bodied K113 F943 RNV. (AS)

Unlike today's Manchester bus scene, for many years the only independent sector competition was between A. Mayne & Son and Manchester Corporation. For years, the bus fleet was entirely of British manufacture, but in 1989 the first of many Scanias entered the fleet in the shape of a pair of Northern Counties-bodied N113DRBs. Appropriately registered 13 (F113 HNC) was the second of the pair to arrive due to requiring modifications after failing its tilt test. (AS)

With the advent of deregulation, Harris of Grays were quick to commence local bus operations under the imaginatively titled Harrisbus banner. Alexander-bodied N113DRB F314 RHK is seen leaving Grays bus station with the State Cinema in the background. Opened in 1938 and able to seat 2,200 people, the cinema's fully illuminated Compton organ rose from the orchestra pit on a lift and was used in the BBC production of *Lipstick on Your Collar*. (AS)

In 1989, in a first for a London buses subsidiary, nine bog-standard Alexander RH-bodied Scania N112s were bought in July 1989 for the London Northern Potters Bar tendered 263 service (Archway station–Barnet Hospital). They moved en masse to MTL in Liverpool in 1996, before moving again to that lover of all things Scania, Black Prince of Morley. The second of the batch, S2 (F422 GWG), is seen en route to Archway when new. (AS)

Caught when being delivered to London Buses is Alexander PS-bodied N113 SA1 (F113 OMJ), one of three vehicles used in comparison trials in their search for a new heavy-duty single-decker, the other two being an Optare Delta and Renault PR100. SA1 wasn't a success in London, and went back to Scania in October 1990, having worked for just over a year and was bought by – yep, you've guessed it – Black Prince. (AS)

At the start of 1994, Leons of Stafford took over PMT's Paramount Leisure coach operation. Vehicles inherited included Van Hool Alizee-bodied K92 5702 PL, new to PMT as F115 UEH and seen here in London in 1995. If I recall rightly (given how long ago it was), Leon's kept the Paramount coaches at PMT's Newcastle depot, and had a Portacabin there to manage the operation. All of the coaches that were transferred (bar one or two) were Scanias. (PG)

Only thirty Scanias were bodied by Duple, all with the low-height 320 body, and 10 per cent of them are seen parked in Bridlington while operating for Wilfreda Beehive of Adwick-le-Street. Right to left, G21 HKY is a K93 new to Wilfreda; F371 CHE is a K92, new to BTS of Borehamwood in 198; and hiding on the left is K92 F89 CWG, also new to Wilfreda, who obviously liked the Scania/Duple combination as they ended up with seven of the thirty. (RS)

The 1990s –
'Money, Money, Money'

The removal of licencing restrictions when the Transport Act (1985) was implemented in October 1986 instigated the biggest shake up in the history of the UK bus industry. Overnight, operators faced competition on their most profitable routes from both new and existing operators, and as a result demand for new buses dropped dramatically – existing operators having to cut costs to ward off the competition, and most of the new operators unable to afford the outlay required to obtain new buses. It also saw the privatisation of the NBC, split into seventy separate companies, many of which were sold to management buyouts. Municipal operators and the PTEs had to be run at arm's length from their local authority, and without the government funding these sectors previously enjoyed they had to rationalise and streamline in order to survive, leaving funding for new buses low on the agenda. London Buses was divided into twelve business units, all of which were sold off between September 1994 and January 1995, and again retrenchment and cost-saving was the order of the day. By the start of the 1990s, a level of stability had ensued, often to the detriment of the new operators, but in some cases to the old established ones, and some famous names disappeared, some through bankruptcy but most due to takeovers, leading to the rapid expansion of the new 'big groups', Stagecoach, Badgerline (later to become FirstGroup) and British Bus (which eventually became Arriva). This stability led to operators shedding the caution of the late 1980s and orders for new buses started to increase. Without the previous restricted buying policies or 'political' buying decisions organisations such as the NBC or PTEs had forced on them, Scania suddenly had access to a much wider market. The N113 continued to be delivered in both double- and single-deck form, and started to enter fleets such as the former London Buses units in substantial numbers. In 1994, it was joined in the UK by the L113, a low-entry step-entrance single-decker chassis with the front section at a similar height to the N113, and an 11-litre engine mounted longitudinally as in the K113 but inclined to the side. This heralded Scania's entry into what was to become the market norm, the low-floor bus. Early examples had bodies by Northern Counties, Alexander and East Lancs; however the most popular body was the Wright Axcess-Ultralow, with FirstGroup taking most of the 330 built.

Back in 1980, Spanish bodybuilder Irizar attempted to break into the UK coach market with the unusually designed Urko, featuring a pronounced 'step' halfway down the body resulting in the rear three windows being about a foot higher than the front two. Fewer than fifteen were delivered and after a further attempt in 1984 with the even less successful Pyrenean, the UK heard nothing of Irizar until 1993 when Scania announced the signing of an agreement giving them exclusive distribution rights for all Irizar coaches in northern Europe, and in 1994 the first Irizar Century-bodied K113s arrived in the UK. Its stylish looks, and features such as powered full-length side lockers, saw the Century become an instant success, entering high-profile fleets such as Bowens, Harry Shaw and The King's Ferry. By the end of the 1980s, nearly 350 Centurys had been delivered to operators in the UK and Ireland, with Bus Eireann making the Century its standard coach.

In 1997 Scania introduced the 4-series, utilising smaller and cleaner engines in order to comply with Euro2 emissions limits. For UK vehicles, all retained the rear-engined layout, with the 'K' series having an upright longitudinally mounted engine, used primarily as coaches, the 'L' having its longitudinally mounted engine inclined 60° to the left, and used for vehicles with low entry but not a full low floor, and the 'N' having a transverse engine inclined 60° to the rear and used for double-deck and fully low-floor, single-deck buses.

Kingston upon Hull's association with Scania went back to the Metropolitan, so it seemed fitting that the last vehicles bought new before the company was sold to Cleveland Transit in 1993 were Scanias, with sixteen of these huge eighty-eight-seat East Lancs-bodied N112s arriving between 1989 and 1990. Seen after sale to Coachmasters of Rochdale is G804 JRH, operating the 456 service between Rochdale and Wigan, a distance of 37 miles, which took somewhere around two and a half hours to do. (AS)

The first of the newcomers to the Liverpool bus scene following deregulation was Liverline of Bootle, formed by a group of redundant Merseybus employees and operating mostly in the south Liverpool area. In 1993 they were bought by British Bus, but not before they purchased ten new Northern Counties-bodied N113s. G38 HKY, new in 1990, is seen passing Liverpool's St George's Hall. (AS)

Above and below: It was announced shortly before I commenced writing this book that the bastion of UK coach tours, Shearings Holidays, had entered receivership. Having operated lightweight Fords for many years, they switched to heavyweights in the early 1980s, subsequently operating most makes of heavyweight chassis. The first Scania arrived in 1990 in the shape of Plaxton Paramount 3200LS-bodied K93 881 (G881 VNA), one of ten delivered that year. In 2001, it was one of two subsequently acquired by Go Goodwin's of Eccles, who dispatched it Blackpool Coach Services where it became the first Paramount 3200 to receive one of BCS's front end facelifts. (AS/PG)

The closest coach company to my home is Happy Days Coaches, who until moving to their purpose-built depot in Stafford, were based in the pretty Staffordshire village of Woodseaves. Always running a fleet of modern vehicles, in January 1990 they purchased five new K93s, three of which were fitted with Plaxton Derwent bodies. Just over a year later, the stage carriage operation was sold to Midland Red (North). G611 CFA is seen in Woodseaves shortly after delivery. (JM)

KM Travel of Lundwood near Barnsley celebrated their fiftieth year of operation in 2021, but I'm sure that if this photograph was taken today, there wouldn't be too much celebrating for the driver seen using his mobile phone. However, back in 2000 when Berkhof Excellence-bodied K93 H3 KMT was in Brighton, the mobile phone laws were still three years away. Originally registered H960 FFW, it was new to Applebys of Louth. (PG)

Above and below: In 1995, West Midlands PTE painted a number of vehicles into heritage liveries. The only Scania painted was Alexander RH-bodied N113 3225 (H225 LOM), which received Birmingham City Transport livery due to its fleet number being the same as WMPTE's preserved ex-Birmingham City Transport Crossley-bodied Daimler. With a cheery wave from the driver, it rounds the now long-gone Manzoni Gardens in central Birmingham. After WMPTE, it was converted to open-top configuration and sold to Guide Friday, subsequently passing to the Bath Bus Company to operate on behalf of City Sightseeing. In 2011 it moved to the exotic climes of Cyprus, and is seen here entering the old town of Pafos having begun its journey at the harbour a couple of miles away. (AS/MH)

In the late 1990s, National Express turned some services into 'Express Shuttles' – passengers just turned up and bought a ticket from the driver via a Wayfarer machine. Shuttle-branded coaches originally received names starting with 'Spirit of…' and ending with a location on the route, and at Wessex where I worked at the time, we had twelve vehicles branded for the Bristol to London and Cardiff services. Down in Kent, the 001 Ramsgate/Margate–London service became a Shuttle, operated by a one-off in the East Kent fleet, very late Plaxton Paramount 3500-bodied K93 8856 (J856 NKK), seen on Lambeth Bridge in 1998. (PG)

In 1992, Shearings was one of the first operators to purchase the new Plaxton Premiere. Unfortunately, issues with build quality, especially with the cantilever-style boot lid which would raise up at speed meant that it was nearly six years before further Plaxton bodies entered the fleet in any large number. The 1992 order included thirty Premiere 320-bodied K93s, and 275 (J275 NNC) sporting Shearings new blue livery is seen outside Battle Abbey. (AS)

In 1992, London Buses received forty dual-door Northern Counties-bodied N113s, which were delivered to East London's Bow depot. Instantly recognisable (well to me anyway) as Aldgate bus station, S66 (K866 LMK) shares space with Leyland Titan T631 (NUW 631Y). (AS)

Seen picking up opposite York railway station is Harrogate Coach Travel's Plaxton Verde-bodied N113 K761 JTV. New in 1991 as an unregistered Plaxton demonstrator, it was the only Scania fitted with a dual-door Verde body. When its demonstration days were over it was converted to single-door layout, registered and joined the Nottingham City Transport fleet. (RS)

Both the remaining Welsh municipal operators favour Scanias, and having seen Newport, it's time for Cardiff. Since 1989 nearly 100 Scanias have entered the fleet, with the first single-deck buses being a batch of fourteen Plaxton Verde-bodied N113s. The first of them was 272 (J272 UWO), seen on Wood Street in Cardiff city centre – I had to check that this was actually Cardiff as every picture of the place I've used in previous books, it's been chucking it down with rain. (AS)

Another double take – at first glance I thought Mary Poppins was walking towards Cardiff's 291 (L291 ETG), then realised it was a window display. The N113 is fitted with an Alexander Strider body and is waiting time in Wood Street, Cardiff. (AS)

Most of my Scania coach mileage was accrued when Western National hired vehicles from Snell's of Newton Abbot to cover for the busy summer season. Snell's had the largest fleet of Scanias in the south-west, including a Scania engined AEC Reliance – an absolute flying machine! Seen at Dover Docks in 1997 is Van Hool Alizee-bodied K113 tri-axle K5 URE, still retaining the private plate fitted by its previous owner Harry Shaw of Coventry. (PG)

Newport also bought Alexander Strider-bodied N113s, including the last Strider to be built. One vehicle from an earlier batch is 70 (L170 EKG), new in 1994 and seen arriving in Newport bus station in 2001. (AS)

When London Country was split into four divisions in readiness for deregulation, London Country (South West) inherited the majority of the London airport services, and in 1989 formed Speedlink Airport Services to encompass the Flightline, Speedlink and Jetlink operations. Seen departing Heathrow is Jetlink-liveried L44 SAS, one of two Plaxton Premiere 320-bodied K93s in the fleet. (AS)

Even though the express rail link between London and Heathrow Airport has operated for over twenty years, the Reading–Heathrow RailAir service is still immensely popular. Back in the 1990s, the service was operated by Q Drive subsidiary Bee Line using Berkhof Excellence 1000-bodied K113s. With the driver patiently waiting while AS gets his shot, 792 (M792 TCF) is seen in Heathrow Central bus station in 1995. (AS)

Above and below: In the early 1900s, Wright's of Ballymena introduced a new range of full-sized single-deck bus bodies, all built to the same basic design, but with differing names for different chassis or floor heights. For the N113CRB, the range included the step-entrance Endurance and for the N113CRL, the low-floor Pathfinder. Midland Bluebird's Endurance 555 (L555 HMS), with Endurance branding on the side panels, is seen waiting time in Edinburgh bus station, while Lowland Scottish 151 (M151 PKS) shares Berwick upon Tweed with a member of the old guard, an Alexander Y Type-bodied Seddon. (AS)

Above and below: The low-floor Pathfinder heralded the start of the new generation of accessible single-deck buses. Despite their Northern Irish registration numbers, the first thirty were delivered to London Buses, and were the only dual-door examples in stage carriage service. They had unusual one-piece front doors, with the wheelchair ramp attached to the centre door as seen on RDZ 1706, departing Turnpike Lane bus station. The Pathfinder also introduced that luxury that we now seemingly can't live without: air conditioning, the pod clearly visible on the roof of First Edinburgh's 568 (M568 RMS), seen travelling down Princes Street in Edinburgh. (PG/AS)

Above and below: East Lancs also went in for virtually identical models in low- and step-floor versions. The low floor MaxCi was fitted to the N113 and L113, but wasn't a success, with only thirteen being built, all delivered to Clydeside 2000. Seen parked at Inchinnan depot are 510/3 (M110/3 RMS). The driver's seats in these buses were air sprung and reputed to be so soft that drivers said if you ran over a postage stamp you'd hit the ceiling. The MaxCi's successor was the European, slightly more successful, running to seventy-nine vehicles, the majority of which were delivered to subsidiaries of British Bus. Departing from my old place of work, Hanley bus station, and heading for my home town of Market Drayton is Arriva Midlands North's 3489 (N429 XRC), new to Derby in 1995. (AS/PG)

In 1986 in readiness for privatisation of the National Bus Company, the northern division of Alder Valley including depots at Bracknell, High Wycombe, Maidenhead, Newbury, Reading and Wokingham was renamed The Berks Bucks Bus Company, trading as 'Bee Line'. The last new vehicles purchased before the company was sold to CentreWest in 1996 were a batch of Northern Counties Paladin-bodied L113CLLs including 817 (M817 PGM), seen parked in Bracknell bus station. (AS)

Another Bee Line, but this time one with some ZZZZs, was Manchester minibus operator Bee Line Buzz, who were taken over by British Bus in 1989, bringing them under the same ownership as North Western. As can be seen by the sticker in the front nearside window, by the time this photograph of Northern Counties Paladin-bodied L113CLL 1042 (P42 MVU) was taken in Liverpool's Hood Street, the group had become part of the Arriva empire. (AS)

England's most westerly operator is Mounts Bay Coaches of Marazion in Cornwall, named after the beautiful Cornish landmark of St Michael's Mount, which sits magnificently behind the company's depot. Owned by the Oxenham family, they began running taxis in the late 1940s before moving onto coaches during the mid-1950s. Mounts Bay are now one of the oldest coach operators in Cornwall and many vehicles in their fleet have OXI cherished registrations reflecting the name of the owners. Most if not all coaches are named and Van Hool Alizee-bodied K113 OXI 626 is called Godolphin Arab. (PG)

Another Van Hool Alizee-bodied K113 is National Express-liveried N683 AHL, owned by The Birmingham Coach Company and seen departing Heathrow Central bus station. As well as National Express contracts, BCC also ran a network of stage carriage services across the West Midlands before selling the near 100 vehicle operation to the Go-Ahead Group in 2005. (AS)

Staying in the West Midlands, we see Flights of Birmingham's Irizar Century-bodied K113 1 FTO. Fitted with only thirty-two seats and kitted out to full executive specification, the coach was used as the Aston Villa team coach and is seen arriving with the team at Wembley for the 2000 FA Cup final. Villa lost 1-0 to Chelsea, but at least they had a nice ride home. (AS)

Northumbria Motor Services was formed in 1986 to take on the Northumberland area routes of United Automobile Services in readiness for deregulation. In 1995, they took delivery of the first of thirty-three East Lancs-bodied Scanias, including thirteen double-deck Cityzens. The name started East Lancs' tradition of using 'misspelt' product names, and the body was built solely on the N113 chassis. 383 (N383 OTY) is seen in Newcastle, turning off Percy Street into Eldon Square bus station. (AS)

Wright's replaced both the Endurance and Pathfinder with the Axcess Ultralow in 1995, all of which were fitted onto L113CRL chassis. The majority were delivered to FirstGroup subsidiaries, including N412 ENW, fleet number 8412 in the Rider York fleet. It is seen in central York when brand new, borne out by the fact that not only are its front fog lights still intact, but it also has the plastic covers attached. (AS)

What I wouldn't give to see a line-up of coaches like this one here again – Berkhof-bodied Leyland Tiger, Bova, Paramount 3500-bodied Volvos, and of course the main focus, Kentish Bus's Wright Axcess Ultralow-bodied L113CRL 255 (N255 BKK). Kentish Bus took delivery of ten of these buses to upgrade trunk route 480 (Dartford to Gravesend). However, on this occasion, the route branding was irrelevant as the bus is travelling down Buckingham Palace Road in London. (AS)

I've always liked the Van Hool Alizee, and long admired the Scottish Citylink livery, so a combination of the two made this a dead cert to be included. Clydeside Scottish K113 N137 YMS is seen in Edinburgh's St Andrew's Square bus station bound for Gourock, one end of what was at one time the longest coach route in the UK, the National Express 547 service from Penzance. (AS)

Seen in Kings Lynn bus station is East Lancs Cityzen-bodied N113 'Fenland Queen' (S333 HEB), the last new double-decker purchased by Fowler's of Holbeach Drove. Fowler's have been serving the community around Spalding and Boston since 1947 and for many years have included operational heritage vehicles in their fleet. (AS)

In 1998, Wright replaced the Axcess Ultralow with the almost visually identical Axcess Floline, although now on the new L94UB chassis. S350 SET as the Scania demonstrator, and after its showing off days were finished, it joined the fleet of Ambassador Travel in Great Yarmouth. (AS)

Further down in East Anglia, we see Eastern National (now First Essex) Wright Axcess Floline 653 L94 (T653 SSF) turning off Colchester High Street into the old bus station. When First initially introduced the purple and pink 'Barbie' livery, it was decreed that it would only appear on low-floor vehicles. (AS)

The 2000s – 'Under Attack'

The ten years from 1999 to 2009 were rather difficult for Scania, seeing three attempts to purchase the company, firstly in 1999 when Volvo announced it was to become the majority shareholder, a move that was later blocked by the European Union. In 2006, German manufacturer MAN tried to acquire Scania outright, later dropping the bid, but increasing its shareholding in Scania to 17 per cent. The third attempt was by the Volkswagen Group, who having already purchased Volvo's share in Scania in 2000, steadily acquired the other major investor's shares resulting in a 71 per cent holding by 2008, and by 2015 Volkswagen controlled 100 per cent of Scania. All this uncertainty and upheaval didn't prevent Scania from making market-breaking decisions, and the decade proved to be the strongest yet in terms of UK and Ireland sales, with nearly 5,000 buses and coaches sold.

The Disability Discrimination Act of 1995 made it law for all new PSVs with over twenty-two seats to be completely low floor from 31 December 2000, and with the introduction of the L94 in 1998, Scania was compliant well before the deadline. A further model was added to the UK low-floor catalogue in 2003 when the first of the fully integral single-deck OmniCitys arrived. Based on the N94 chassis, the OmniCity was Scania's first full low-floor bus, and since 2006 has been built at Scania's plant in Słupsk, Poland. Also introduced was the OmniLink, outwardly similar to the OmniCity, but with a step access to the rear due to its engine being longitudinally mounted. The OmniCity was also available as an articulated bus, but didn't sell in large numbers in the UK market. Despite an articulated demonstrator touring London in 2004, the London order went to the Mercedes-Benz Citaro, and the fifty-nine articulated OmniCitys delivered to the UK could only be found in Heathrow Airport, Manchester, Cardiff and Birmingham. The N113 was still available in the UK for fitting with double-deck bodies until 2000, Scania being rather late to the party in building a low-floor double-deck chassis. However, this changed in 2002 when the N94UD was introduced. Initially it was only available with modified East Lancs Myllennium bodywork, fitted with the front end cowl and windscreen from the OmniCity and in keeping with the 'Omni' theme was marketed as the OmniDekka. It became popular across the UK, being purchased by the big groups including Stagecoach and, from 2005, FirstGroup, who had failed to get Wright, their preferred bodybuilder, to body the N94UD, citing body to chassis weight distribution issues with the double-deck Gemini body. The same year, Scania launched a fully integral double-deck version of the OmniCity, and as a result the OmniDekka was removed from general sale with vehicles only being built for existing customers. Someone in Scania's development team must have had a crystal ball, as in 2007 East Lancs collapsed, the assets of the company eventually passing to Optare who discontinued building body-on-chassis vehicles. The OmniDekka was not the only Scania/East Lancs collaboration, as in 2002 a batch of shortened N94UB chassis was fitted with single-deck Myllennium bodies for delivery to London Easylink. Named the OmniTown, it retained standard Myllenium front and rear panels until 2004 when the OmniTown received front and rear panels from Scania to match the OmniCity and OmniDekka.

On the coach side of things, the 2000s were exciting times for Scania. Having previously worked with Plaxton to produce the Expressliner during the 1980s and 1990s, National Express turned to Portuguese bodybuilder Salvador Caetano to build a coach body exclusively for National Express to allow the company to comply with the Disability Discrimination Act of 2005. The Caetano Levante enabled wheelchair passengers to access the coach via the front door using a front-mounted lift. The first Scania chassis to be fitted with the Levante (and in fact the first Scania chassis to receive any Caetano body) was delivered in 2006, and to date nearly 500 Scania/Levantes have been supplied to National Express contract operators. Also in 2006, Scania announced an agreement to work with Finnish bodybuilder Lahden Autokori Oy ('Lahti') to build the OmniExpress semi-integral coach. The Irizar agreement from the 1990s remained, the range increasing to include the low-height Intercentury semi-luxury coach and the educational transport specific S-KOOL.

In 2006, the 4-Series was replaced by the current K-Series and N-Series, and as with the 4-Series, all vehicles for the UK and Ireland are rear engined. The K-Series replaced the K94, K114, K124 and L94 and has its engine longitudinally mounted. European Emission Standards define the acceptable limits for exhaust emissions of new vehicles sold in the European Union, and when first introduced, the K-Series was offered with a Euro IV-compliant 8.9-litre engine with power outputs between 230 bhp and 310 bhp and an 11.7-litre engine with power outputs between 340 bhp and 470 bhp. The N-Series replaced the N94 and has a transversely mounted engine with power outputs between 230 bhp and 280 bph and is used on all low-floor buses, whether single or double deck. N-Series variants are the 'UB' two-axle single-decker, 'UA' tri-axle articulated, and 'UD' two-axle double-decker. In 2008 Scania upgraded the Euro IV engines to Euro V, with the 8.9-litre engine increased to 9.3 litres, and the 11.7 litre to 12.7 litres.

Having such a huge interest in the company, I will always try to include a Yelloway coach in my books wherever possible, but with the original Yelloway company's policy of always buying British. Had they still been operating, I wonder what vehicles they would have in the fleet today? The 'new' Yelloway, part of Chadderton-based Courtesy Coaches, has no set buying policy, and in 2009, the registration Y15 YEL was being carried by Irizar Century-bodied K124, new to Durham Travel Services as T12 DTS. Hopefully the driver noticed the lack of nearside headlight unit... (PG)

Colin Spratt started operating coaches from the Norfolk village of Wreningham in the 1940s, and the company served the wider community for nearly eighty years until closing the doors in 2018, the cost of meeting the London ULEZ regulations cited as one of the main reasons. Spratt's always had a tidy fleet, with many coaches purchased new, the last one being Van Hool Alizee T9-bodied L94 W27 GES, seen visiting Lincoln Christmas Market. (PG)

First introduced into the UK in 2002, the OmniCity is an integrally constructed bus built at Scania's plant at Slupsk in Poland. The first UK orders were delivered to Nottingham City Transport and included FD02 SEY, which subsequently became WX 6025 with Connexionsbuses of Tockwith in North Yorkshire. Seen outside York railway station, it is branded for the Ebor Connexion route between Wetherby and York. Ebor is the abbreviation of the Latin Eboracum, the early name of York in Britain. (RS)

Staying in Yorkshire, we head to the pretty town of Thirsk. For over ninety years, Reliance Motor Services of Sutton on the Forest have been running bus services into York from the wider North Yorkshire area. Wright Solar-bodied L94 NL02 ZRX leaves the bus stand in Thirsk Market Place, the bus unusually retaining the red livery of its previous operator Go North East. (RS)

With over 500 bought since 1999, Bus Eireann (Irish Bus) must be one of the world's largest operators of Irizar-bodied Scanias. One of the many liveries used is that of C.I.E. Tours, Córas Iompair Éireann being the holding company of Bus Eireann, Dublin Bus and Iarnród Éireann (Irish Rail). New in 2001, L94 SC5 (01-D-27583) is seen travelling down Dublin's O'Connell Street Lower. (AS)

Seen in East Croydon in the early hours of New Year's Eve was PG's last steed of 2015, ex-Metrobus OmniCity YN03 WRL. Now operated by Southern Transit of Brighton, it had just operated a rail replacement service for Southern Railway from Three Bridges and Gatwick Airport. (PG)

The next four photographs show Wright Solar-bodied L94s from Wellglade Group subsidiaries, starting with Trent's 609 (FJ03 VVX) wearing the two-tone purple Pronto livery for the service between Nottingham, Mansfield and Chesterfield. Wellglade was formed in 1986 when Trent was purchased from the National Bus Company in a management buyout. (RS)

Having started as a coach operator in the 1970s, Gilbert Kinch of Mountsorrel in Leicestershire commenced operating local bus services in 1987 under the Kinchbus brand. At the start of the 1990s he began to expand around Leicestershire and Nottinghamshire before selling out to the Wellglade Group in 1998. Seen about to depart Nottingham's Broadmarsh bus station is 623 (FJ03 VWN). (RS)

I'm sure someone once told me that Crystal Peaks was an actor in films you wouldn't show your gran, but we all know its's actually a shopping centre in Sheffield. Suitably liveried for Sheffield Line 30, TM Travel's 635 (FJ03 VXC) is seen passing Sheffield Town Hall. (RS)

Caught turning in Rutland Square in the picturesque town of Bakewell is TM Travel's 601 (FJ03 VVN), liveried for the Peak Line 218 between Sheffield and Bakewell. TM Travel was founded in Chesterfield in 1995 as a family-owned operation running one coach. A move into local bus services saw the fleet increase to over 100 vehicles in just over ten years, making it Derbyshire's largest independent operator before being taken over by Wellglade in 2010. (RS)

From the avalanche of operators who began operating Continental shuttle holidays at the start of the 1980s, Siesta Holidays of Middlesbrough are one of the few still undertaking this work. The current fleet consists of Van Hool deckers, but back in 2003 you could be whisked off to Spain on Berkhof Axial 100-bodied K114EB6 V16 SCC, new to Siesta and originally registered YN53 PBX. (RS)

The driver of Coach Innovations' TUI 4857 obviously knows how important RS is – who knows, maybe he'd bought one of my earlier books featuring RS's work? Originally registered YN53 GDX, the identical sister ship to the coach above was taking a party of Rotherham United supporters to Wembley where Rotherham won the League One playoff to gain promotion to the Championship apparently, as I have no idea what any of that means... (RS)

While Scania were quick to provide chassis for low-floor single-deckers, they were very late to the party with a double-deck chassis, so much so that in 2002, East Lancs bodied a batch of short wheelbase N94UB chassis with their standard Myllennium body. A year later, after consultation with Scania, the OmniDekka was launched, consisting of a modified Myllennium body fitted with the front end from the OmniCity. Seen freshly repainted in Yorkshire Traction's traditional red and cream livery is Stagecoach Yorkshire 15414 (YN54 VKD), new in 2004 as Yorkshire Traction 804. (RS)

Compared to other major UK cities, Bristol's buses have seen relatively little competition, with the first serious attack on the incumbent operator coming from Abus, founded by former Badgerline manager, Alan Peters, in 1991. Abus had the honour of putting the first fully low-floor double-decker into UK service but suffered an arson attack in 2009 that destroyed much of the fleet. One casualty of the fire was East Lancs OmniDekka-bodied N94UD BU54 AJP, new to Abus in 2005. (PG)

Staying with Bristol operators, we see Turner's Irizar PB-bodied K114EB 73 WAE passing Bath Abbey in the pouring rain. Turner's depot's close proximity to Bristol Temple Meads railway station has meant that for decades they have been the 'first-call' operator when emergency rail replacement coaches were needed, so much so that at one time drivers would be put on night standby waiting for the call to assist. (RS)

With Kernow branding, First South West's Wright Solar-bodied L94 65764 (YN05 GXO) seems a little bit lost as it travels through Glastonbury in 2018. Unusually for FirstGroup, this bus was bought second hand, being new to Reading Buses, but was purchased to operate the Truro Park & Ride, hence the Kernow branding. (PG)

During my time at First PMT, the full-sized single-deck bus fleet was entirely Scania, with the majority of vehicles cascaded down from other FirstGroup companies. New to the company, however, were two batches of OmniCitys, which were allocated to Adderley Green depot and used on the flagship 101 service between Hanley and Stafford. 65027 (YN05 HCL) has since been repainted in the retro post-privatisation livery and is seen leaving Hanley bus station. (PG)

As well as the OmniCitys, First PMT also received eighteen Wright Solar-bodied L94s, which were shared between the Wirral and Potteries divisions. Seen as the early morning sun rises on a foggy Sunday morning is 65731 (YN05 HCX), the driver taking advantage of the lack of passengers to pop to the Co-op on Liverpool Road in Kidsgrove. (MH)

If there was an award for the body with the most different sized windows, it would surely have to go to the OmniTown, the name given to the 'midibus' length N94s bodied by East Lancs. Some were fitted with front panels from the East Lancs Esteem body, as seen here on YM55 SXB. New to Metrobus for the Grove Park–Lewisham routes 181 and 284, they only seated twenty-nine passengers. Subsequently sold to Trustybus, it is seen in Loughton. (PG)

The OmniTown was also available with Scania front and rear panels similar to the OmniCity and OmniDekka but with a flatter front end and was available in lengths of 9.1 metres up to 10.8 metres. Nottingham City Transport's 205 (YN04 ANP) was one of a batch of seven originally used on tramway feeder services. (RS)

It was 2003 before the first articulated OmniCitys arrived in the UK for car park shuttles at Heathrow Airport. In 2004, an N94UA demonstrator toured London but failed to win any orders, losing out to the Mercedes-Benz Citaro but did gain orders from Travel West Midlands, Cardiff Bus and First Manchester. One of the latter was 12007 (YN05 GYE), bought for use on the Manchester–Bury corridor. (RS)

Thamesdown Transport (now known as Swindon's Bus Company) ran a number of Lunchtime Link services to bring employees of the many large companies based on the outskirts of Swindon into the town centre at lunchtime. Seen undertaking such a duty is OmniDekka 377 (YN55 NHL), new to London United in 2005 as SLE17. (RS)

Seen passing Network Rail's former Western Region headquarters, 125 House, is Thamesdown Transport's 509 (WX06 JYA), a Wright Solar-bodied L94 delivered new in 2006. Thamesdown remained in municipal ownership until 2016 when it was sold to the Go-Ahead Group. (RS)

Clowes Coaches, based near Leek in the Staffordshire Moorlands, have owned tri-axle Irizar PB-bodied K114 VRY 1X since new in 2006. Seen on tour in Scarborough, it was originally registered GC06 GKC, its current registration plate was originally fitted to a Smit-bodied DAFs, Clowes operating one of the handful of Smits imported into the UK in the 1980s. (RS)

Based on the Intercentury, the low-height version of the Century, Irizar's S-KOOL was developed specifically for educational transportation. All built on the L94 chassis, they were normally fitted with seventy belted seats in a 3+2 configuration, the majority being painted bright yellow when new. YN05 HFW was new to Lugg Valley of Leominster and is seen on Rylands Road in its home town. (RS)

Brighton & Hove's policy of naming vehicles after people who have made significant contributions to the city included Samuel Lewis, one of Britain's richest men when he died in 1901. He supported the convalescent hospital at Black Rock and the Royal Sussex County Hospital, and is commemorated on OmniDekka 682 (YN57 FYM), seen on Queens Park Road in Brighton. (PG)

The wonderfully liveried Yorkshire Tiger's roots are in the Calderdale area operations of Yorkshire Traction, and despite not carrying corporate identity is part of Arriva. Originally SO6 in the Transdev London United fleet, there is no indication at all that East Lancs Olympus-bodied N23OUD 905 (YN07 LHW) was built new as a dual-door bus. (RS)

Another orange East Lancs Olympus-bodied N230 is 9195 PU from the Wheelers of North Baddesley fleet, one of four acquired from Reading Buses. Originally YN08 HYM, it is seen with another of the batch on rail replacement work at Southampton Central, their eighty-seat bodies making them ideal for this sort of work. (PG)

DM58 DRM of Herefordshire operator DRM of Bromyard is proof that providing a quality product reaps rewards. New to DRM in 2009, while it looks like a tri-axle OmniCity, it is in fact an OmniLink, the main difference between the two being that the chassis on the OmniLink has its engine longitudinally mounted, meaning a step to access the rear portion of the saloon. It is seen travelling up The Homend in Ledbury on DRM's core service to Hereford. (RS)

Above and below: Despite Portuguese-built Caetano coachwork being available in the UK since the late 1960s, it wasn't until 2006 that the first were put onto Scania chassis. The Levante was designed specifically for National Express to comply with the Disability Discrimination Act of 2005, and used a front-mounted lift to allow wheelchair passengers to enter the vehicle via the front door. Silverdale of Nottingham are one of several independent operators undertaking NatEx contracts, and FJ09 DXU, seen departing Sheffield Interchange, was purchased new. NatEx imposes age restrictions on vehicles used on the network and by 2016, FJ58 AKU, new to South Gloucestershire Bus & Coach, had been sold to Eirebus, re-registered 08-D-126453 and used on the Swords Express service. (PG)

PG wasn't expecting to see a Gasch when he popped along to Canterbury in 2019, but there was this nice big one. With a full-sized fleet made up almost entirely of Irizar PB-bodied Scanias, Autocares Gasch is one of the oldest family operated coach companies in Spain, boasting nearly ninety years of operation, and their vehicles are regular visitors to the UK undertaking work for Panavision Tours. (PG)

When captured on camera in Salisbury in 2019, Go South Coast subsidiary Wilts & Dorset's 1145 (HW09 BBZ) was looking extremely smart for a ten-year-old bus. Liveried for the company's Salisbury Reds operation, the differences between this double-deck OmniCity and the previous photographs of OmniDekkas is clear, the offside mounted engine of the OmniCity preventing the fitment of a window in the rearmost bay. (PG)

Like Wilts & Dorset, Southern Vectis is also a subsidiary of Go South Coast, hence the closeness of the fleet and registration numbers between the two OmniCitys on this page. Both were part of a batch of twenty-one OmniCity deckers delivered to the company in 2009, eleven of which were allocated to Southern Vectis for services on the Isle of Wight, and 1149 (HW09 BCO) is seen picking up in Ryde en route to East Cowes. (RS)

Despite bodying some of the first BR112s in 1982, Alexander didn't body any Scanias between 1997 and 2008. Having now become part of Alexander Dennis, the Enviro 400-bodied N230UD became popular in certain Stagecoach fleets, including Stagecoach East Midlands, whose 15510 (FX09 DAA) is seen leaving Gainsborough bus station. It carries a special version of Stagecoach livery for Lincolnshire InterConnect services. (RS)

Seen leaving the Yorkshire Wildlife Park is Mayne of Manchester's Irizar i4-bodied K310 54 (YT09 FMC). The i4 replaced the InterCentury and can be configured so that the centre door can have a wheelchair lift fitted. (RS)

2010s – 'Super Trouper'

This final chapter brings the Scania story in the UK and Ireland up to the present day. In 2013, Scania introduced its new range of Euro VI engines and the 9.3-litre engine's power outputs now range from 250 bhp to 360 bhp while the 12.7-litre outputs range from 410 bhp to 490 bhp. As the European Emission Standards become stricter, engine manufacturers have had to find new ways to meet their targets, and while Scania has been using exhaust gas recirculation (EGR) and selective catalytic reduction (SCR) systems, alternative fuels are also available including compressed natural gas (CNG) and ethanol. A CNG-powered double-deck version of the N-Series chassis was launched in 2016, fitted with Alexander-Dennis Enviro 400 bodywork, and by the end of 2019 that stalwart of Scania operators, Nottingham City Transport, had over 120 in service. A year earlier, in 2015, the double-deck OmniCity was phased out, leaving the Enviro 400 as the only double-deck body fitted to N-Series chassis.

While the tie-up with Irizar continues through to the present day with the i6-bodied K-Series seen as the flagship of the Scania range, the future of the OmniExpress was cast into doubt in 2013 when Lahden Autokiri filed for bankruptcy. All the existing orders were satisfied and in April 2014 Scania announced that it would take over the production plant in Lahti. In 2015, OmniExpress production did come to a halt when Scania announced that the Lahti plant would start to build a new coach named the Interlink. Powered by either the 9.3- or 12.7-litre engines and able to run on ethanol, CNG or diesel, the Interlink was designed to be a fully versatile vehicle, available in three heights and any length between 11 and 15 metres. 2014 was a busy year for Scania when it was announced that the Chinese-built Higer Touring HD would be made available to UK operators. Scania and Higer had been working together since 2005 and introduced the Touring in 2007. By the end of 2014, over 500 Tourings had been delivered across Europe and the initial batch of twenty chassis for the UK were sold before they were even imported.

The Oxfordshire town of Wallingford is a mystery lover's paradise, for not only did Agatha Christie live there for over forty years, *Midsomer Murders* aficionados will recognise it as Causton, the capital of Midsomer County and the town where the show's main characters lived and worked. Seen passing through is Oxford Bus Company's Enviro 400-bodied N230 220 (JF10 OXF), on hire to fellow Go-Ahead subsidiary Thames Transit. (PG)

Talking of The Oxford Bus Company, they took the only Plaxton Panther-bodied Scanias, a batch of eighteen K360s in 2011, all with consecutively lettered 'OXF' registration plates. In 2017, 18 (UF61 OXF) was transferred within the GoAhead Group to Plymouth Citycoach, Plymouth having just taken on some Majestic tour work, on which the coach can be seen visiting Lewes. Sadly, in July 2020, Plymouth Citycoach was disbanded, a victim of the Covid-19 crisis. (PG)

In 2007, Scania announced a tie-up with Finnish coachbuilders Lahden Autokori Oy to build semi-integral coaches known as the Scania OmniExpress. The first UK examples arrived in 2010 and included YR20 BFX, new to Premier Connections, Luton Airport, but seen here on Hino Travel work with Little's of Ilkeston. Lahden filed for bankruptcy in 2013, and a year later Scania announced that it was taking over Lahden's former factory in Lahti to continue building the OmniExpress. (RS)

The Scania/Irizar tie-up continued despite the collaboration with Lahden, with the i6 becoming the flagship of the range. Ulsterbus have operated nearly 250 Irizar-bodied Scanias, the current 'prides of the fleet' being three 13.5-metre-long K440s allocated to the Ulsterbus Tours department. Irizar i6 134 (FFZ 9134) is seen a long way from home parked in Boppard in the Rhine Valley. (PG)

One of the most stunning photos I have seen for a long time is this shot of Stagecoach Devon's N230 ADL Enviro 400 15801 (WA61 KZM) travelling down Torbay Road in Torquay. With PG making good use of the high vantage point on Livermead Hill to take the photo, the tempestuous sea whipping across the road contrasting with the genteel splendour of The Royal Terrace in the background. (PG)

Staying with the stunning shot theme, MH was enjoying the view of the rolling hills above the picturesque Cumbrian village of Grasmere when what should go and add to his enjoyment but Stagecoach Cumbria's ADL Enviro 400-bodied N230 15726 (PX61 CVF). The livery blending nicely with the background is no coincidence, buses working the 555 service between Keswick and Lancaster wear a green version of Stagecoach livery. (MH)

Living in rural North Shropshire we're not exactly overrun with coach operators, so when hiring coaches for things like school trips, Happy Days of Stafford are usually first choice, however it probably wasn't the best idea to hire them to take mourners to a recent funeral. Seen at speed on the M1 taking Sheffield Wednesday fans to the 2016 Championship play off is Irizar i6-bodied K400 226 (YP12 NRF). (RS)

The modular construction of the Scania chassis allows for special build vehicles such as the four short 10.7-metre Irizar i6-bodied K360s built for City Circle of London, specialists in incoming tourist work as evidenced by the Globus logo on the side of the coach. These vehicles are perfect for smaller groups who demand the comforts of a full-sized coach, and 78 (YT13 HLD) is seen outside the Ashmolean Museum in Oxford in 2014. (PG)

Stagecoach Devon's Big Beach Bus plies its trade between Sandy Bay and Exmouth using Enviro 400-bodied N230 15665 (WA10 GHG), which had an altercation with a low bridge in Royston when operating with Stagecoach Yorkshire resulting in its conversion to partial open top. Seen on Exmouth sea front, the thrill of the open top doesn't seem to have attracted too many punters. (PG)

In 2018, Worthing Coaches took over the contract for the University of Brighton shuttle service and made SC13 BUS, one of only a handful of Irizar i3s in the UK, the dedicated vehicle. Seating forty-four, it often gets overloaded, hence it being stalked by a more luxurious member of the Worthing fleet. The bus was new to Scania (UK) and was the i3 demonstrator. (PG)

Recent years have seen a huge upsurge in the numbers of CNG (compressed natural gas) buses on the road, with Stagecoach, Nottingham and Reading leading the way. Seen in Bracknell bus station is 425 (YN14 MXU), one of the latter's ADL Enviro 300-bodied K270s. I was going to say how well applied its 'Leopard' livery is, even going some way towards incorporating the roof-mounted gas tanks, then I noticed the decapitated leopard towards the rear... (PG)

With the statue of Steve Ovett getting a bird's-eye view of Vallance of Annesley Woodhouse's Irizar i6-bodied K360 V6 LLN, RS's vantage point allows us a view of the roof-mounted Hispacold air-conditioning system. New to Solus of Tamworth in 2013 registered YT13 AMV, it is caught on camera parked on Brighton sea front. (RS)

Not only has Stagecoach West Scotland's VCS 376 received the registration from an original Western SMT bus (ECW-bodied Bristol FLF B1822) but it was chosen to receive traditional Western SMT livery complete with period fleet number KC689. An Enviro 300-bodied N230, it was originally registered YN64 AHA and is seen leaving Glasgow. (PG)

For such a popular body, there have been fewer than fifteen Van Hool-bodied Scanias delivered to UK operators in the past decade. A long way from home is Amport & District's WA15 BWC, a Van Hool Alicron-bodied K360, seen arriving at the Yorkshire Wildlife Park. (RS)

Above and below: Built in the fourteenth century, the impressive Crown Spire of St Giles' Cathedral keeps a watchful eye on Omega's Higer Touring-bodied tri-axle K410 YT15 AWJ as it travels down Lawnmarket on Edinburgh's Royal Mile. In the lower picture, with the massive changes to the industry caused by the Covid-19 pandemic, never has the slogan on the side of Higher-bodied demonstrator YT19 DYN been truer! Seen on hire to Corbel of London, it is arriving at Bedford on rail replacement duties. The Higer, the flagship of the Scania range, is built in China, and is the latest tie-up between Scania and a bodybuilder, with the first of nearly 200 examples imported into the UK in 2015. (PG)

Formed in 1926, South Notts Bus Company of Gotham operated a service between Nottingham and Loughborough until the company was sold to Nottingham City Transport in 1991. Following the takeover, South Notts' name and livery was retained for vehicles operating the Loughborough service. Seen on Carrington Street in Nottingham, passing one of the best kebab shops I've ever been in, is Enviro 400-bodied N230 644 (YN15 EJE). (RS)

Despite only being on sale in the UK for nine years, the Lahden OmniExpress racked up fairly impressive sales figures, with some high-profile fleets taking multiple examples. One such fleet was Harry Shaw of Coventry, who ordered seven, with KOV 1, KOV 2 and 84 COV arriving in 2015. KOV 1 is seen on Church Way in Doncaster with the Minster Church of St George in the background. (RS)

Above and below: TrawsCymru is the brand name for a network of medium and long-distance express bus routes in Wales. Sponsored by the Welsh government, it was introduced in 2011 as a replacement for the TrawsCambria network by providing improved connections, and operators would be awarded contracts to run a service for a prescribed number of years. The T3 from Wrexham to Barmouth was initially awarded for seven years to GHA Coaches, but following GHA's collapse in 2016, it was taken over by Lloyds of Machynlleth, whose Enviro 400-bodied SN15 ETF is seen leaving Barmouth. The T4 runs from Newtown to Cardiff, and is the longest journey in the network with a run time of nearly four hours. It is operated by Stagecoach Red & White and Enviro 300-bodied K230 28734 (YN15 KGG) is seen departing Brecon en route to Cardiff. (MH/RS)

Baker Dolphin's Gold Service tour programme is operated by a small fleet of Irizar PB-bodied Scanias, all with appropriate BD GLD registration numbers. With RS getting a cheery smile from the driver and courier, BD15 GLD pulls away after a stop in Chesterfield. (RS)

The subtle design differences between Irizar's PB and i6 can be compared on this page. Formed in 1949 as Wilfreda Luxury Coaches, by acquisition of companies such as Roeville and Fagre, Wilfreda Beehive have grown to become one of the largest operators in South Yorkshire. Seen emerging from under Doncaster's Frenchgate Shopping Centre is i6-bodied K410 YR16 BKL, one of a pair purchased new in 2016. (RS)

Out of the fourteen Van Hool-bodied Scanias delivered to UK operators since 2011, three of them went to Leons of Stafford. Seen on the same football supporters job as the Happy Days coach in picture 151 (Leons owning Happy Days Coaches) is Van Hool Alizee-bodied K360 AT65 LCT. (RS)

In 2015 Scania announced the Interlink as the replacement for the OmniExpress. Built at the former Lahden plant in Lahti, the semi-integral coach is available in two- or three-axle configuration, and can be powered by diesel or CNG. One of the first in the UK was YN66 WSF, new to Milligan of Mauchline for operating contract tours for Caledonian Travel. It is seen arriving in Brighton. Is it just me or does it bear more than a passing resemblance to the first Scania coach imported into the UK back in 1973? Either way I'm not sure about the shape of those wheel arches. (PG)

Like they say, 'if it ain't broke, don't fix it'. Until the introduction of the Levante 3 in 2018, the original Levante saw very few styling changes, as can be seen when comparing Skill's of Nottingham's BD65 JFG from 2015 with the pair seen earlier in this book. Picking up in Chesterfield, it is operating the 310 service, which runs between Bradford and Southsea and clocks up over 300 miles each way. (RS)

After a gap of nearly ten years, National Express reintroduced double-deck coaches onto its network when six Caetano Boa Vista-bodied K410s were supplied to Edwards Coaches of Llantwit Fardre, initially for use on the Bristol–London corridor. These were the first double-deck Caetano coaches imported into the UK and included BV66 WPK 'John', seen in Weston-super-Mare. (PG)

Brentwood Coaches have served the good people of south-west Essex for over fifty years, and recently introduced an all-over silver livery to replace the previous white, yellow and brown stripes. Seen in Shanklin Old Village on a tour of the Isle of Wight is Higer Touring YR16 BNY. (PG)

Also seen on the Isle of Wight, but in Sandown is Irizar i6-bodied K360 YS16 LNC operated by Solus of Tamworth, an operator whose fleet has consisted predominantly of Irizar-bodied Scanias for over twenty-five years. (PG)

Now you'd think this would also be on the Isle of Wight seeing as it's carrying IOW Tours livery, but Travelstar of Gatwick's OmniExpress YN66 WRV is actually pulling away from Brixham on the Devon Riviera. Despite the gloriously sunny backdrop, the photo was taken on a cold crisp November's day. (PG)

Currently only one of two coaches in the UK carrying contract livery for American tour operator Tauck is City Circle's Irizar i6-bodied K410 YN16 WUH. In the background is Conwy Castle, built by Edward I during his conquest of Wales between 1283 and 1289, and considered by UNESCO to be one of the finest examples of late thirteenth- and early fourteenth-century military architecture in Europe. (PG)

Stagecoach East Kent's Enviro 400-bodied 15329 (YN67 YLB) is painted in the group's new Azure blue Local Service livery, introduced at the start of 2020 in an attempt to make it easier for passengers to identify their required service. Proudly proclaiming that it 'runs between Eastbourne and Hastings' as it's coming through Hailsham, it appears to have somewhat failed in its task. (PG)

Reading Buses operate the largest fleet of Irizar i3s, with six fitted to K250UDs purchased in 2017 to operate the Vodafone contract. 26 (YN17 ONL) is seen in Newbury when brand new. (PG)

Vehicles from the fleet of Johnsons of Henley-in-Arden dominate this 2018 Stratford-upon-Avon scene. Until 2000, Johnsons concentrated purely on coach hire, but stepped in to cover contracted work for Warwickshire County Council following the failure of the incumbent operator, and today Johnsons operate nearly thirty routes across the West Midlands. Seen running back to the depot after a school run is Interlink YN17 OMT. (PG)

Similar livery, opposite end of the UK. Seen in Princes Street, Edinburgh, undertaking Scottish Citylink duties is Edinburgh Coachlines' tri-axle Irizar i6-bodied K410 YR68 VMF. Edinburgh Coachlines are now a subsidiary of Eirebus, having been formed over forty years ago as Silver Fox Coaches with a base just a mile from the centre of Edinburgh. (PG)

Nowadays it seems that route branding rather than corporate livery is the order of the day for the big groups, especially FirstGroup. Seen departing Peterborough bus station for the 80-mile-plus journey to Norwich is First Eastern Counties Alexander Dennis Enviro 400 City-bodied N250UD 36914 (YN69 XZU). I can only assume there is plenty of intermediate passenger flow to warrant running double-deckers on a service frequency of thirty minutes on a journey of this length. (RS)

Based in Coimbra, Portugal, MOBIpeople was formed from the ashes of the European arm of Brazilian coachbuilder Marcopolo. BASE Coach Sales, Marcopolo's former UK importer, approached MOBIpeople with a brief to build a PSVAR compliant two-door seventy-seater coach, complete with air conditioning and good luggage capacity. The result was the attractive-looking Explorer, initially only available on MAN chassis, but now also available on Scania. Seen on its first day in service is Weavaway's YN20 YLA, seen in Bicester undertaking rail replacement work. (PG)